YULETIDE HEARTH

Christmas in an 1806 Pennsylvania Farmhouse

Yuletide Hearth
Christmas in an 1806 Pennsylvania Farmhouse
Text © 2002 by Katharine Z. Okie
Photography © 2002 by Blair Seitz
and Katharine Z. Okie
ISBN 1-879441-97-7

Published by

RB

BOOKS
Harrisburg, PA

Seitz & Seitz, Inc.
1010 North Third Street
Harrisburg, PA 17102
www.celebratePA.com

Designed by Klinginsmith & Company

Printed in China by Regent Publishing Services
St. Louis, MO 63123

Yuletide Hearth

"
Look now! For glad and golden hours
Come swiftly on the wing;
O rest beside the weary road
And hear the angels sing!"

-Edmund Hamilton Sears

KATHARINE Z. OKIE

PHOTOGRAPHY BY AUTHOR AND BLAIR SEITZ

I wish to express my gratitude to the following people who helped me bring this book to fruition.

To my late husband, Howard, who found this house for us, and shared with me his love of music, early American architecture, history, antiques, country life, children, animals, and Christmas. His affections are reflected in this book. ✺ *To our children, Edward and Spencer, with whom we shared our Christmases throughout the years, and who continue to enrich my life. I treasure their support of this effort, which was needed and lovingly given.* ✺ *To Blair Seitz of RB Books, who was attracted to the book's concept, and agreed to publish it. The addition of his own outstanding photographs to those of this amateur has contributed significantly to its visual beauty.* ✺ *To Cheryl Klinginsmith, the book's Art Director and Designer, whose creative talent is evident throughout.* ✺ *To my Editor, Eleanor Boggs Shoemaker, whose proficient observations, thoughtful guidance, persistent encouragement, and warm friendship were invaluable.* ✺ *To my mother, Mary Amory Zantzinger, whose love of reading and literature made her an ideal "sounding board" early in the project, and whose interest and support were constant from start to finish.* ✺ *Most hymn and carol lyrics are taken from The Hymnal 1940, and The Hymnal 1982, of The Episcopal Church of the United States of America. Biblical passages are from the King James Version of The Holy Bible.* ✺*Lyric excerpts of "White Christmas" by Irving Berlin, © Copyright 1940, 1942 by Irving Berlin, © Copyright renewed; International copyright secured; All rights Reserved. Reprinted by Permission*

Table of Contents

SWEET CHRISTMAS! The holy season filled with memories and hope, whose meaning and magic are annually rediscovered through our senses, hearts, homes and history.

Its two great stories capture the imagination and the spirit; the amazing account of Jesus' birth, and the tale of generous Saint Nicholas' Christmas Eve journey.

Its observance evokes thoughts of home and hearth, a house and its occupants, partners in celebration.

Houses built long ago that have survived the march of time, bestow upon their families special gifts, and, at Christmas, take on a magic all their own. Perhaps it is the accumulation of so many "Christmas Pasts" that brings every "Christmas Present" an added measure of warmth and peace. Through window and door, its images reflect the quiet serenity born of time's passage. Their unpretentious aura rekindles the commonplace, allowing us to perceive anew the subtle beauty in the everyday world.

Christmas has a mysterious way of stringing the years together, anchoring each twelve-

month strand with a hopeful beginning or reverent end. In old houses, that garland is very long, weaving through the rooms with a pattern unique to a place with a lengthy history. Along it are threaded the memories, daily events, and Yuletide celebrations of the people whose lives unfolded, and continue to unfold, within its walls.

This is the story of my 19th century home's garland: the families it has sheltered for nearly 200 years, and historic events that marked their tenure. Pictures, and quotations from verse, song and Scripture narrate the two thousand year old Christmas message which has inspired and uplifted the lives of its occupants as America evolved from a cluster of colonies to nationhood and world prominence.

Chester County, Pennsylvania is a region renowned for impressive 18th and 19th century manor houses, elegant homes of the landed gentry, the politically powerful, and the scholarly elite. Compared to those architectural treasures, this old farmhouse is humble indeed. But from Philadelphia's Main Line to the Lancaster County border, the Schuylkill River to the Delaware State line, the County is dotted with hundreds of similar modest dwellings. These were home to the average men and women who pioneered rural America.

In the early 1800's, occupants of these buildings were called" yeomen", an expression left over from the English class system. The term was apt. Webster's defines yeoman as " a man of the commonality of the first and most respected class; a freeholder; one who cultivates

Now to the Lord
sing praises,
All you within this place,
And with true love
and brotherhood
Each other now embrace;
This holy tide of Christmas
Doth bring redeeming grace.

O tidings of comfort and joy,
Comfort and joy;
O tidings of comfort and joy!

LONDON CAROL, 18TH CENTURY

his own farm." The adjective, yeomanly, is defined as "brave, rugged, staunch, sturdy".

Usually located at the western edge of white settlements, such houses often evolved from log structures that, over time, were refined with native fieldstone and stucco by their increasingly affluent owners: the farmers, smithies, tradesmen, and merchants who flooded the fertile lands first bought from William Penn's administrators.

These intrepid English, Scotch, Irish, Welsh, and German immigrants came to Pennsylvania to exercise religious freedom, surely making their first Christmas in America an event of unprecedented significance.

The Christmas season heightens my awareness of the subtle, lingering presence of the yeomen families who lived here. Somehow the old stonewalls seem to echo their prayers and songs, laughter and weeping. At times I pause in the quiet and think of them, attempting to penetrate the density of time to share their Yuletide experiences, stringing them together with mine.

I behold images they too would have seen; trees trimmed with cherished ornaments; festive holiday tables luminous with candlelight, awaiting the sumptuous bounty of hearth and oven; stockings hung in the mantle's shadow obese with surprises obscured in tissue paper; swirling snowflakes falling past hand-blown glass window panes.

Familiar sounds continue to echo through the house; children's laughter, timeless carols, the door latch clicking as guests enter, friendly voices calling greetings, firewood snapping and

crackling. All this is sensed and seen enveloped in the pungent elixir of pine and balsam, cider, cinnamon, mint, fresh baked bread and cookies.

Resting by the fireplace, whose 21st century use is now primarily decorative, but was for previous families the core of life and survival, I ponder the Yuletide history that has unfolded near its hearth, binding all the occupants together as participants in America's story, and man's quest for peace on earth, good will among men.

It began the year Lewis and Clark's Corps of Discovery returned safely from exploring the western lands acquired by President Thomas Jefferson, when two courageous, enterprising women began their own microcosmic version of that adventure, initiating the first crude settlement on the softly rolling hills and meadows I view each day.

Christmas 1806

IN SEPTEMBER 1806, Ann and Elizabeth McCrosky, Scotch-Irish spinster sisters, came from Uwchlan Township, part of the famous Welsh Tract west of Philadelphia, to an 86-acre parcel of raw wilderness land to farm and raise flax. With winter approaching, they hastily built a tiny log house for shelter, the farm's first structure.

What must they have felt that Christmas night as they huddled alone by the fire, facing their first winter on the yet unproductive little farm?

Coming to the land late in the year, there was just enough time to cut sufficient wood to get through until spring, but no crops could be harvested, and records show they had only one cow, protected by a crude lean-to stable.

However, they had no fear of Indians, for the Lenni-Lenape, who once moved so freely about the region, had long since departed, leaving their ancestral lands to the determined settlers.

Preparing for Christmas worship, they could have drawn upon a Presbyterian, Catholic, or Quaker tradition, the faiths of other widely scattered homesteaders in the area. We don't know which it was. But within their primitive shelter on the tiny parcel of Pennsylvania frontier, they surely asked for God's protection, feeling as alone as Mary and Joseph in their Judean stable. PERHAPS THEY COMFORTED EACH OTHER BY SINGING:

Inspite of a vulnerable beginning, the sisters survived the first winter, and succeeded in their farming enterprise. By Christmas of The War of 1812, they had "plow land divided into small fields...a good bearing orchard with excellent fruit...milk cows, young cattle, sheep, and swine; grain in the ground, rye,

"He came down to earth from heaven,
Who is God and Lord of all,
And his shelter was a stable,
And his cradle was a stall.
With the poor, the scorned, the lowly,
Lived on earth our Savior holy.."

ONCE IN ROYAL DAVID'S CITY
BY CECIL FRANCIS ALEXANDER

corn, and potatoes by the bushel;...about 200 lbs. of flax from the break, and the same quantity swingled; a quantity of fine and course tow; a quantity of flax and tow yarns prepared for weaving; a large quantity of course and fine sewing thread prepared for market.." [1]

But after eight years of strenuous work, Ann and Elizabeth's progress was suddenly halted and Christmas 1814 was their last. It

THE MCCROSKY SISTERS' COTTAGE - 1806

must have been a dismal Yuletide. Records show they both died in early January 1815 within five days of one another.

What happened to these industrious women? How did they die at virtually the same time? Perhaps an accident or contagious illness cut short their remarkable saga. But respect for their endurance and achievements are a vivid, continuing legacy.

Often, as I walk through their little house, or wander over the land they worked so hard, or see the remnants of their fine orchard, I remember them; honor their struggle, and their short lived, yet very real, successes.

They are forever a part of Christmas here.

[1] Newspaper Estate sale notice- February 1815

Christmas 1823

THE NEW OWNERS of the McCrosky homestead observed Christmas with gratitude, and a sense of accomplishment. In 1819, the year Spain ceded Florida to the United States, Jacob Baum bought the farm from the McCrosky estate, moved his wife and sons into the log house, and began to build. During the next four years they constructed a stone farmhouse, and shortly thereafter, added a wing with its own cooking fireplace and stair, providing more privacy for his eldest son and wife.

The log lean-to was replaced with a substantial stone barn, and the log house and crude frame structure protecting the spring were also reconstructed in stone. Such building proclivity, matched with their industrious work on the farm, leads me to believe the Baum's may have been Amish or Mennonite.

In 1823, the family moved to the new house in time for the holidays, and enthusiastically celebrated the season, grateful to be out of the confined quarters of the cottage.

During the next two years they busied themselves with crop production, and Jacob Jr. pursued his weaving trade, which was housed in the McCrosky cottage. Like the sisters, he too raised flax for linen.

Because of their comparative isolation, the family was probably little affected by the

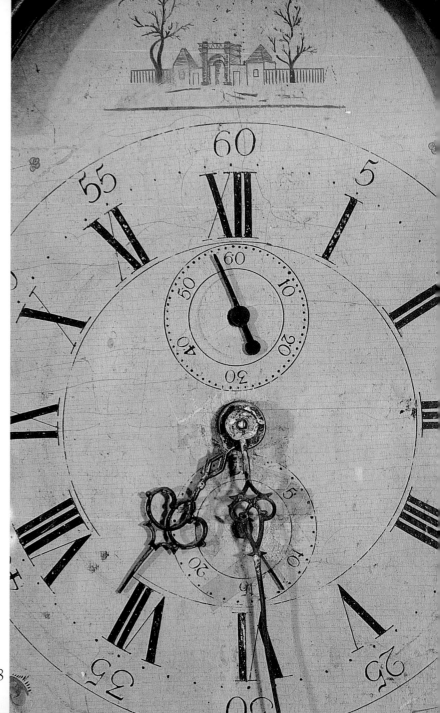

18

major events of their time: Andrew Jackson's stormy Presidency, the fall of the Alamo, the tragic removal of eastern Indians to the Oklahoma Territory along the infamous Trail of Tears.

Jacob Sr. died in October of 1824. Christmas that year would have been subdued, pervaded by feelings of loss and remembrance. But if his death were a release from an affliction, the family could commit his soul to God's care with a phrase from a new Christmas song written two years earlier, and destined to become ONE OF THE WORLD'S MOST BELOVED CAROLS:

"..*Sleep in heavenly peace.*
Sleep in heavenly peace."

FROM *SILENT NIGHT*
BY FRANZ GRUBER

Jacob Jr. took title to the farm following his father's death, and prospered another 19 years. When they sold the farm in 1843, the Baum family had passed 24 Christmases within the walls of the stone farmhouse they had built with such skill and care.

I often think of them when gazing through the blown glass windowpanes they set with their own hands, or as stockings are hung above the same fireplace

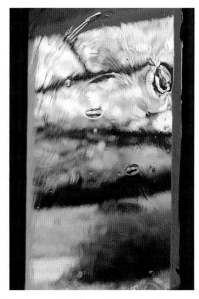

two generations of Baum children hung theirs.

Christmas 1846

I N 1846, DAVID AND ANNE JEFFRIS, took title and celebrated the first of 30 Christmases at the farm. Sitting around the table of their new home, they would have been hard pressed to imagine the turbulent times that lay ahead for the country during the next two decades.

As they were enjoying the settled stability of their lives, the Oregon Trail was funnelling thousands across the continent toward land in Oregon, Washington, and California. Many started their trip along the Lancaster Turnpike that passed only three miles south of the farm, moving along the "improved" toll road in Conestoga wagons, a design unique to the region from which they took their name. Further west they were called "prairie schooners" as they wended their way on and on, leaving Pennsylvania and the Jeffris family far behind.

Its easy to envision Mrs. Jeffris going to nearby Downing's Town and watching these great caravans roll by as she shopped for supplies to make holiday gifts; some fabric for a dress, yarn for a sweater. Did she feel admiration for their courage, or distain for their foolhardiness?

Guiding her buggy back up the lane to the farm, she was probably glad that her Christmas would be spent settled and safe, not toiling through the Allegheny Mountains in the dead of winter, lurching toward an unknown, inconceivably distant destination. Or might a part of her been secretly excited by the thought of such mad adventure?

By the Christmas of 1849, gold had been discovered in California, further unleashing the frenetic movement west. Being so near the pioneers' route, younger members of the Jeffris family might have been tempted to join the great exodus in search of excitement and wealth. It must have been hard to keep farm boys home that year.

Christmas in the 1850's

THERE WERE NUMEROUS EVENTS to trigger conversation around the Jeffris Christmas table throughout this decade; the flood of immigrants filling eastern ports with refugees from the potato famine in Ireland and reports of the brewing hostility between pro and anti-slavery factions in the newer states and territories of the west.

Slavery was a topic of considerable concern in the region surrounding the farm. The Chester Valley was filled with Quakers who were active and dedicated abolitionists. There, private homes and Friends Meetings served as stops on the Underground Railroad, enabling runaway slaves to reach freedom. We don't know the Jeffris' views on this issue, but it's possible that, in 1852, a copy of Harriet Beecher Stowe's newly published bestseller, *Uncle Tom's Cabin* could have been under their Christmas tree.

As the family gathered to pray for "Peace on Earth, Good will to men" in 1859, could they have suspected that the country was about to be torn apart by its bloodiest war?

Christmas in the 1860's

It would be intriguing to know specific details of this period in the Jeffris' lives. The Civil War was raging. Surely family members, perhaps even Jeffris sons and brothers, had left their farms to fight for the Union. Fear and hardship were swirling all around them. In December 1862, Christmas was marred by the dreadful news of the slaughter of Union troops at Fredericksburg, and six months before Christmas 1863, the war had come as close to the farm as Gettysburg. It seemed that a VERSE FROM THE CAROL "I HEARD THE BELLS ON CHRISTMAS DAY" was sorrowfully accurate for the farm's inhabitants during those holiday seasons:

..."But in despair, I bowed my head
There is no Peace on Earth I said.
For hate is strong, and mocks the song
Of Peace on Earth, Good will to men."

In 1865 the Jeffrises gathered at a Christmas feast marked by joy and grief. The War had ended, the Union saved, slaves freed. The slaughter was over. But now the casualty list of 600,000 American souls included Abraham Lincoln. This was a loss northern citizens of the mutilated nation found almost impossible to bear, having come to love and revere him. In April, many members of the farming community had gone to Downingtown to watched respectfully when his funeral train made a brief stop there.

In spite of their bereavement, by Christmastime it was probably possible for them to sing the last verse of " I Heard The Bells...." with some modest conviction:

"So peal the bells more loud and deep.
God is not dead, nor does he sleep.
The wrong shall fail, the right, prevail,
With Peace on Earth, Good will to men."

-HENRY WADSWORTH LONGFELLOW

However, the next few decades would test the farm's occupants' belief that peace on earth was anywhere near at hand. Others having the same difficulty would be citizens dealing with the enormous problems of Reconstruction, black and white. But those who would give up on that hallowed hope completely and forever would be the American Indians.

Christmas 1876

In 1876, A NEW FAMILY congregated at the farm for the festive Centennial holidays and they stayed for 49 years, longer than any other family to date. The Jeffris had sold the property in 1868 to Esau Loomis but held the mortgage for the transaction. When David Jeffris died in 1875, Mr. Loomis was unable to purchase the farm outright necessitating a Sheriff's sale to settle the estate. Henry and Ann Lewis bought the farm for $4925.

The Lewises spent the spring and summer planting and tending crops. Over the years, the farm had expanded to 108 acres. With such a large parcel requiring their attention, the Lewis children, John and Mary, undoubtedly worked alongside their father and mother.

As they settled at the table for the first Christmas Eve meal in their new home, Mr. Lewis, a devout Methodist-Episcopalian, probably offered an appropriate seasonal blessing.

"With all Thy Hosts,
O Lord, we sing,
Thanks and praise to Thee we bring,
For Thou,
O long expected guest,
Hast come at length
To make us blest."

FROM THE CHRISTMAS ORATORIO

BY J.S. BACH

When dinner was concluded, older members of the family would move to the hearth, drawing their chairs near the fire for a final cup of hot cider. Conversation may have turned to a trip to the Centennial Exposition in Philadelphia, which the Lewises could have taken since railroad spurs now served rural communities.

Pavilions at the Exposition showcased industrial, technical, and agricultural inventions that were sweeping the country. Two that may have been of particular interest to farmers were Alexander Graham Bell's first-prize winning telephone, and the Central American exhibit featuring an exotic fruit called the banana.

Within a few days of the country's birthday celebration on July 4, news of Custer's Last Stand at the Little Big Horn was reported in Philadelphia newspapers sending shock waves through the city and countryside. Cries arose throughout the nation demanding a "final solution" to the Indian "problem". Ann and Henry may have shared that view, but perhaps they longed instead to honor the message of the man whose birth they were celebrating that night: "Good will to ALL men, all men, all men..."

As adult fellowship continued late into the night, the Lewis children, long since in bed, were thinking only of Santa Claus. Like so many other boys and girls, who, over the years, had climbed the little winding stairs to the chilly rooms above, they too could smell wood smoke from the fire, the spicy, sweet fragrances of apple pie and pudding, and hear the muffled murmur of conversation, laughter, AND AN OCCASIONAL CAROL:

"*The snow lay on the ground,*
The stars shone bright,
When Christ our Lord was born
On Christmas night.
Venite adoramus, Dominum
Venite adoramus, Dominum......."

After placing a protective banking of ashes around the Yule log, their parents also retired. Drawing quilts close to their chins to keep out the draft, the family wished each other good fortune, health, and harvests in the years ahead. Then through the darkened second floor, a gentle call:

"MERRY CHRISTMAS CHILDREN." "MERRY CHRISTMAS PAPA." "MERRY CHRISTMAS MAMA." a wish repeated over the years.

29

"'Twas the night before Christmas...
"...When all through the House,

Not a creature was Stirring,
Not even a mouse..."

..." The stockings were
hung by the chimney with care,..."
"In hopes that Saint Nicholas

Soon would be There..."

FROM A VISIT FROM ST. NICHOLAS

BY CLEMENT CLARK MOORE

Christmas in the 1880's

During the 1880's, Ann and Henry were securely settled on the farm, blessed with a moderate climate and fertile lands. To be sure, agriculture continued to be a demanding enterprise, filled with strenuous labor and long hours. But it was nothing compared to the struggles of their fellow farmers on the Great Plains, who battled blizzards, grasshoppers and drought.

The West was exploding in many ways. Beef was the new crop. Range wars and cattle drives gave rise to different types of American heroes and villains, such as Wyatt Earp, Bat Masterson, and Billy the Kid.

Colonel William Cody, known as Buffalo Bill, brought the West to Chester County when he chose two farms near the Lewises to winter some of the livestock from his famous Wild West Show.

During the Christmas holidays of 1886, the family probably drove their sleighs the short distance to one of the farms, and watched Cody return with the animals from a performance at Madison Square Garden, part of the festivities celebrating the Statue of Liberty's dedication in New York Harbor.[2]

By Christmas 1887, Ann and Henry had achieved sufficient affluence to build a large addition to the farmhouse, giving them two new parlors for receiving quests over the holidays.

Dashing through the snow,
in a one horse open sleigh,
O'er the fields we go,
laughing all the way!
Bells on bobtails ring,
making spirits bright,
What fun it is to ride and sing
a sleighing song tonight!

JINGLE BELLS
-JAMES PIERPONT, 1850

[2]History of East Brandywine Township by Barbara Paul 1992

Heated by Franklin stoves, considered a refinement over fireplaces, the new, warm rooms were ideal places to play games, sing and read together.

Dickens' A Christmas Carol, was a story they may have shared that Yuletide. By the 1880's the book about Ebenezer Scrooge and the Cratchet family was popular in America

❧

" . . . .There never was such a goose. Bob said he didn't believe there ever was such a goose cooked. Its tenderness, and flavor, size and cheapness, were the themes of universal admiration. . . Then the pudding was out of the copper. . . . Oh, a wonderful pudding! Bob Cratchet said, and calmly too, that he regarded it as the greatest success achieved by Mrs. Cratchet since their marriage. Then all the Cratchet family drew round the hearth in what Bob Cratchet called a circle. . . . And at his elbow stood the family display of glass: two tumblers, and a custard cup without a handle. These held the hot stuff from the jug, however, as well as golden goblets would have done; and Bob served it with beaming looks, while the chestnuts on the fire sputtered and cracked noisily.

Then Bob propsed:
"A merry Christmas to us all my dears. God bless us!"
God bless us everyone!" said Tiny Tim. . . ."

From A CHRISTMAS CAROL – Charles Dickens

and its importance in Christmas celebrations would grow. Many years later it became a cherished ritual of my own childhood Christmas Eves. The tree trimmed and stockings hung, my Mother, Father, sister and I always ended the evening in a glow of fire and candlelight, listening to Ronald Coleman's eloquent, gentle voice narrate the tale on 78 rpm records.

1888 brought furious winter storms. In the East, from Washington to northern New England, the largest snowfall on record, still known as the Great Blizzard of '88, paralyzed cities and surrounding countryside.

Without television weather channels or radio meteorologists to alert people of impending freaks of nature, the first flakes could be precursors of a two to forty inch snowfall. No one knew. But as people of the land they took what came, probably feeling far less anxiety than we, with all our forewarning, information and statistics.

Throughout farming communities such weather was not a great concern as long as haylofts and granaries were full, wood cut, and sufficient food canned in the fall. When paths were dug to the barn, springhouse and out house, morning and evening chores com-

pleted, the balance of the time could be spent in restful, companionable pursuits. There was no way to plough roads and no cars to dig out. If it were necessary to leave home when the storm had spent its fury, a sleigh or good horse provided the means. But mostly one simply stayed put.

Twenty years earlier, in his great winter elegy Snowbound, New England poet, John Greenleaf Whittier recorded his childhood memories of family life while confined indoors during snowstorms. The Lewises undoubtedly experienced the simple pleasures it describes, as we did one hundred years later. Hidden somewhere in the words of that touching poem may well be nestled the beginnings of the nostalgic yearning for a "White Christmas".

..."All day the gusty
north-wind bore
The loosening drifts its breath before;
Low circling round its southern zone,
The sun through dazzling
snow-mist shone..."

"...As night drew on, and from
the crest
Of wooded knolls that ridged the west,
The sun, a snow blown traveler, sank
From sight beneath the
smothering bank..."

"..We piled with care,
Our nightly stack
Of wood against
The chimney back....."

"..then, hovering near,
We watched the first
red blaze appear
Heard the sharp crackle,
caught the gleam
On whitewashed wall
and sagging beam,
Until the old,
rude-furnished room
Burst, flower-like, into
rosy bloom.
Shut in from all the
world without,
We sat the clean-winged
hearth about,......."

...Content to let the north wind roar
In baffled rage at pane and door...

...While the red logs before us beat,
The frost-line back with tropic heat....
The merrier up its roaring draught
The great throat of the
chimney laughed.
The house-dog on his paws outspread
Laid to the fire his drowsy head

The cat's dark silhouette on the wall
A couchant tiger's seem to fall;
And, for the winter fireside meet,
Between the andirons straddling feet,
The mug of cider simmered low,
The apples sputtered in a row,
And close at hand the basket stood
With nuts from brown
October's wood....

....Sit with me by the homestead
hearth,
And stretch the hands of memory forth
To warm them at the wood-fire's
blaze!...

FROM <u>SNOWBOUND</u>
BY JOHN GREENLEAF WHITTIER

Christmas 1899

THE LAST CHRISTMAS of the 19th Century must have been especially festive, with more than usual attention given to detail: extra baking, additional pine boughs throughout the house, harness bells polished, and sleigh horses groomed to perfection.

During church services, along with the usual carols, prayers and songs honoring the past and blessing the future were likely said and sung:

"O God, beneath thy guiding hand
Our exiled fathers crossed the sea;
And when they trod the wintry strand,
With prayers and psalms they worshipped thee.

Laws, freedom, truth, and faith in God
Came with those exiles o'er the waves;
And where their pilgrim feet have trod,
The God they trusted guards their graves.

And here thy Name, O God of love,
Their children's children shall adore,
Till these eternal hills remove,
And spring adorns the earth no more."

-LEONARD BACON, 1833

As the Lewises prepared to greet 1900, anticipation must have been tinged with historical perspective. The last time a century passed away, the farm's hills and meadows were wooded wilderness, and America was a small cluster of colonies, just beginning its great experiment with democracy.

More recent events that caused reflection included the Johnstown flood, and the murder of the great Sioux chief, Sitting Bull, who had traveled with Buffalo Bill's show. A new movement afoot in the nation had women discussing Women's Suffrage. Sooner than she wished, rights of women would gain special relevancy for Ann when Henry died suddenly in 1901. As widow Lewis, she learned to manage her affairs well enough without him to stay on the farm another 24 years.

"Deck the Halls
With boughs of holly,
Fa,la,la,la,la,la....
'Tis the season To be jolly!
Fa,la,la,la,la,la....
Don we now,
Our gay apparel
Fa,la,la la,la,la...
Troll the ancient
Yuletide carol!
Fa,la,la,la,la....

Fast away the old year passes.
.Fa,la,la,la,la,la,....Hail to you
Ye lads and lasses.
Fa, la,la,la,la,la,..
Sing we joyous,
Altogether,Fa,la,la,la,la,la,...
While I tell of
Yuletide treasure!
Fa,la,la,la,la...La,la,la,la."

Christmas 1918

"..Let every house be bright
Let praises never cease:
With mercies infinite,
Our Christ hath brought us peace!"

-HOWARD CHANDLER ROBBINS

$\mathcal{P}$EACE! The word had not generated such rejoicing at Christmas since the close of the Civil War. In November 1918, World War I ended in victory. The nation's involvement had been brief but bloody.

During the war years, Widow Lewis would have heard the whistle of Troop trains passing through Downingtown carrying draftees to Philadelphia. Now they were bringing husbands, sons, and brothers home in time for Christmas.

The night of the Armistice, parades and dancing spontaneously erupted in Downingtown's streets, and surely Ann, her children and grandchildren, must have been part of the throng. It was the perfect way to start the holiday season. Closing my eyes, I can almost hear the town's church bells ring-ing; and from all directions, spilling over the hills and sliding through notches to the valley floor, the deep-toned farm bells tolling their own simple salute to peace.

$\mathcal{B}$ONG.....BONG.....BONG.....

Christmas continued to be celebrated at the farm. To assist his mother, John may have been living there with his family allowing Ann time with grandchildren, instructing and modestly spoiling them, as grandmothers are prone to do. They must have been particularly precious to her during the holidays.

She was grateful for basic country pleasures just outside the door for their enjoyment: sledding on a Flexible Flyer, skiing while being pulled by a horse, (called yoring), snowball fights and snowman building.

Inside, sweet apples from the orchard and nuts from the walnut tree embellished the hearth. Simple gifts still filled hand-knit stockings. Children persisted in seeking loving

"And there were in the same country, shepherds abiding in the field, keeping watch over their flocks by night. And lo, the angel of the Lord came upon them, and the glory of the Lord shown round about them, and they were sore afraid. And the angel said unto them: "Fear not! For behold I bring you good tidings of great joy which shall be to all people. For unto you is born this day, in the city of David, a Savior, which is Christ the Lord. And this shall be a sign unto you: Ye shall find the babe wrapped in swaddling clothes lying in a manger". And suddenly there was with the angels a multitude of the heavenly host, praising God and saying: "Glory to God in the highest, and on earth, peace, goodwill toward men."

LUKE 2:8-14   KING JAMES BIBLE

47

arms and laps while listening to carols and Bible readings.

For the remaining seven years of her life Ann watched the world around her change dramatically from anything she or her for-bearers had known. The "Roaring '20's gave birth to a popular culture defined by excesses. Radio, movies and magazines preached the doctrine of "Ain't we got fun?", extolling extravagance and self indulgence. To help bring restraints to a society some perceived to be out of control, Ann, a Methodist, may have been involved with the Women's Temperance League, achieving some success in 1920, when Prohibition became law.

Ann Lewis died in 1925. Perhaps because of the economic pressures facing farmers the children sold the farm, ending their chapter in its history.

At Christmastime I think of the Lewis' nearly half-century here, and their lives and revelries during the holidays. The sound, before dawn, of footsteps crunching through snow on the way to the barn; the cattle lowing as they, in turn, hear footsteps approaching; the "ping" milk makes as it hits the pail; roosters crowing; hens squawking as eggs are stolen from beneath them; the quiet munching of horses eating hay and grain; not really so different from any other farm day.

But upon returning to the house things begin to change. As the door opens the smell of apple fritters, pancakes, bacon, sausage and scrapple collide and mingle with bitter cold air tinged with the scent of wood smoke from the fire. This intoxicating blend signals that the day is different indeed. It is Christmas Day.

Father back, and chores completed, the children know they can bring their stockings to the breakfast table to squeeze and poke, but not open until the meal is over. On it goes throughout the day until the sun sets, night descends and Christmas, once again, draws to a close.

Somehow, I am a part of it all, though separated by so many, many years.

"All my heart, this night rejoices
As I hear,
Far and near,
Sweetest angel voices.

"Christ is born,"
Their choirs are singing,
Till the air
Everywhere
Now with joy is ringing."

-Paulus Gerhart, 1656

Christmas in the 1930's

WHEN THEY PURCHASED THE FARM in 1925, Isaac and Alice Hall became its last farming family. Their sixteen-year tenure was a struggle for survival as the nation was capsized by the Great Depression and then frantically sought to right itself. Few others were more adversely affected by the economic disaster than farmers.

The Halls were fortunate in securing a mortgage before the Stock Market crashed in 1929. Following that horrendous event, many small, rural banks failed having overextended credit to farmers who were unable to meet payments because of low crop prices. By 1932, the per capita income from agriculture was as little as $80 a year.

During those hard times Isaac and Alice fed the family their own milk, eggs, fruits and vegetables from the farm. In this respect they were marginally better off than people in business or manufacturing. Hundreds of thousands of those ended up in bread lines. The only Christmas sentiment to cling to during that era was the original one: hope for the future.

In the early 1990's , one of the Hall's two daughters, Mildred, visited me and gave a first person account of their life here. In spite of the hardship that was rampant throughout the nation, her memories of home and childhood were fond ones.

She and her sister Helen, like most children in those days, were generally content with what they had as long as it included love, family stability and enough food and shelter to keep the hunger pangs and cold at bay. In the '30's there was still no electricity on the farm. News of what the "haves" had, and what one "should want to have too", was largely lost to them. As with the Lewis children, the simple, at-hand pleasures were sufficient to keep them occupied. One of Mildred's favorite pastimes was having breakfast in the meadow where she gathered wild strawberries to add to her bowl of Rice Krispies. (The strawberries still grow there).

Isaac was a dairy farmer but his herd was small, only about 10 cows. Mildred said her father was so tenderhearted that he wouldn't raise pigs or sheep; the inevitable slaughter being something he preferred to avoid. His animals were regarded with some affection, and seen as partners in his agricultural enterprise.

It's easy to imagine the two girls bundling themselves against the cold on Christmas morning and running to the barn to offer the work horses, Prince and George, and the wagon horses, Dolly and Smart-Ass Fred, treats of apples and a handful of grain to mark the occasion.

I can envision them commandeering a small section at the end of the hay trough to recreate their own nativity tableau: A doll is wrapped in homespun; Mildred and Helen taking turns being Mary or Joseph; a family dog or two, or three ordered to sit at dignified attention to be the Wise Men; and, of course, the bovine cast is near at hand; a pack of barn cats dart about, then stopping, stare vacantly at the unfamiliar scene. The girls appoint them sheep.

Though cold outside, the barn is warmed by the cows bodies and breath. Windows drip with condensation; the moisture enhancing the sweet smell of hay. The sense of shelter and safety is all around.

The Hall's, like most farmers, struggled to overcome the realities of the crippled economy. Isaac regularly took milk to the nearby creamery in his run-about. The Model T and Model A Ford remained idle in the wagon shed due to the high cost of gasoline. To supplement their income, two bedrooms in the Lewis wing were periodically rented; one to Hannah Harner, the schoolmistress of the one–room school

"Away in a manger,
No crib for a bed,.
The little Lord Jesus
Laid down his sweet head.
The stars in the bright sky
Looked down where he lay,
The little Lord Jesus
Asleep on the hay.

The cattle are lowing,
The baby awakes,
But little Lord Jesus
No crying he makes...."

-TRADITIONAL CAROL

"In the bleak mid-winter, frosty wind did moan.
Earth stood hard as iron, water like a stone.
Snow had fallen, snow on snow,
Snow on snow on snow;
In the bleak mid-winter, long ago."
In the bleak mid-winter, a stable place sufficed,
For the Lord God incarnate, Jesus Christ."

-Christina Rosetti, 1872 Carol

over the hill. Industrious Alice and Mildred went to work in Downingtown to lend further support to the family.

Celebrating Christmas those years must have required philosophical perspective. Many, like <u>A Christmas Carol's</u> Cratchet family, attempted to make much of the little they had, trying to believe that "less was more", perhaps even sufficient. For the Halls and others, the "grinch" of the Depression may even have reawakened the real meaning of the Holidays.

And from church pulpits, then as now, came the WORDS OF THE GREAT CHRISTMAS PROPHESY OF ISAIAH to reassure them:

Comfort ye,
Comfort ye
my people.........."

"He shall feed his flock
like a shepherd;
And He shall gather the
lambs with his arms
And carry them in
His bosom,
And gently lead those that
are with young...

-ISAIAH

. . .It is coming, Old Earth, it is coming tonight!
On the snowflakes which cover thy sod.
The feet of the Christ-child fall gentle and white,
And the voice of the Christ-child tell out with delight
That mankind are the children of God. . .

"The feet of the humblest may walk in the field
Where the feet of the Holiest trod,
This, then, is the marvel to mortals revealed
When the silvery trumpets of Christmas have pealed,
That mankind are the children of God.

-PHILLIPS BROOKS

Upon his election in 1932, Franklin Roosevelt initiated programs to address unemployment and poverty. In an effort to assist farmers, Congress passed the Agricultural Adjustment Act and the Work Projects Administration. But for Isaac and Alice, help from these programs came too late. The WPA brought electricity to rural areas, solving the problem of refrigeration for dairymen. But in 1937, when it was finally available at the farm, the Halls had already lost their little herd to tuberculosis. In 1941, their mortgage was foreclosed and attempts to succeed on the farm came to an end.

At Christmastime, recalling their years here, I feel a special admiration for Isaac and Alice. They were the 20th century equivalent of "yeomen": "brave, staunch, and sturdy", committed to doing what was necessary to endure, no matter how difficult. Yet, they didn't quite make it. The times were against them. Perhaps even Isaac's tender-hearted nature undermined his success as a farmer. But they stand out for their integrity, courage, and persistence in the face of probable defeat. Heroes by virtue of effort, they represent the honest, able "also-rans" of the human experience, and I salute them. They will always be a valued part of the farm's "Christmas Past".

Christmas In The 1940's

THIS DECADE MARKED the beginning of the property's transition from a working farm to a home for professional families. The metamorphosis began in the spring of 1941. Dallas Pratt, a New York City psychiatrist practicing at Bellevue Hospital, and his friend John Judkin, an Englishman active in The American Friends Service Committee, sought a country retreat where they could find relief from urban pressures. Acquaintances in the Friends Meeting in Downingtown urged them to look for a place in Chester County.

A realtor was commissioned to find an affordable older property. Dallas Pratt recalled driving down the road and seeing a farm that had clearly fallen on hard times. But it was situated on open, rolling land, and the house had a modest beauty in spite of its neglect. He realized immediately that it was what they had been looking for.

Not needing the crop fields, barn, or granary, the men sold them to the neighboring farmer, retaining the house, ten acres, and a tiny tenant house Jacob Baum Jr. had built in the 1830's.

John and Dallas promptly began the task of refurbishing the dilapidated buildings. Following structural repairs, the house was fitted with indoor plumbing and electricity for the first time, and given a name: BRANDYWINE FARM.

As the holidays approached, they looked forward to their first Christmas in the country, but, on December 7, their anticipation was tarnished by the attack on Pearl Harbor. War was immediately declared against Japan and seven months later against Germany, which was plundering Europe and bombing England.

As a British subject and Quaker, John found these years extremely trying. Concern for the defense of his country and the pacifist teachings of his faith caused him ambivalence and anguish. Action was the answer to his pain. He traveled abroad with the American Friends Service Committee assisting its refugee program; including an attempted rescue of 2000 Eastern European Jewish children from Hitler's demonic plan.

Dallas joined the Army as a Colonel, ministering to the psychiatric needs of soldiers and officers.

Between the demands of these commitments, the men were able to proceed with the restoration. Both were antiques enthusiasts and frequently traveled abroad in quest of furniture and paintings. Consequently, the house, once such an unpretentious dwelling, reflected their eclectic tastes. Ornate appointments included one room featuring 17th century wallpaper from a French villa.

A plan to convert the McCrosky cottage into a small regional museum featuring Chester County antiques and artifacts was conceived. Over the years, it had been used for a variety of farm related activities such as a rendering room for making scrapple and apple butter and, most recently, a summer kitchen.

"O come, thou dayspring
from on high,
And cheer us by thy drawing night;
Disperse the gloomy clouds of night,
And death's dark shadow
put to flight.......

O come, Desire of nations bind
In one the hearts of all mankind;
Bid thou our sad divisions cease,
And be thyself our
King of peace........"

FROM VENI EMMANUEL, 1710

They gutted its interior in preparation for the improvements and constructed an enclosed passageway connecting it to the main house.

Throughout the war years they always returned to the farm for Christmas. Surrounded by friends from New York and Downingtown, they celebrated the holidays enfolded by the gentle hills and quiet of the countryside, far removed from the stresses of world conflict.

But radio and newspapers precluded complete detachment from world events. Edward R. Morrow's nightly broadcasts from London covered the Nazi's bombing of the city, and a week before Christmas 1944, the bloody Battle of the Bulge. Reports revealed the full extent of the Holocaust, and the staggering civilian toll of America's agonized choice to deploy the Atomic Bomb.

61

God rest ye merry, gentlemen,
Let nothing you dismay!
Remember Christ our Savior

.

Was born on
Christmas Day!
To save us all from
Satan's power
When we were gone astray,
O tidings of comfort and joy
Comfort and joy!
O tidings of comfort and joy!

However, since the Christmas message is especially relevant in horrific times, Dallas and John continued to gather with their friends to trim the tree, play their favorite holiday games, dine, and go to Meeting; holding onto faith in the power of the manger to triumph over all the bombs, guns, cannons, and spears of human history.

During Christmas 1945, an air of heartfelt festivity at Brandywine Farm finally prevailed. For the war had ended on both fronts. Now the men were free to turn their attention to an idea that had evolved while working on the Cottage. They still wanted to open a museum featuring American decorative arts but decided it should be in England. In 1950, they committed to that course, sold the farm to their friends, Marnie and Ben Schauffler, returned to New York and devoted their energies to raising money for the project. Six years later the dream became reality when the now famous American Museum at Claverton House in Bath was opened.

Dallas and John's contributions to this house remain all around me. The value they placed on indigenous American architectural design and their restrained restoration of the building during its modernization, retained its modest, warm persona. I am grateful for those sensitivities, when, at Christmas, I remember the influence other occupants have had on the evolution and preservation of this dear place.

Christmas in the 1950's

JOHN JUDKIN AND THE SCHAUFFLERS became acquainted through their mutual involvement in the American Friends Service Committee. During the War years, Dallas and John rented the Schaufflers the farm's tiny tenant house. Their daughter, Jing Lyman, then a college student, recalls the building's dilapidated condition and all that was done to make it habitable. It was little more than three rooms stacked on top of each other; the ground floor had been used to house chickens. One fireplace was the only source of heat. After enormous effort, Marnie, Ben and Jing were able to convert the primitive building into a livable home.

Their friendship with Dallas and John deepened as they became part of the Brandywine Farm community, and shared involvement in the AFSC's work, particularly, the Eastern European Refugee Program in which John and Marnie were active.

When the men decided to leave the farm in 1950, the Schaufflers purchased it, and lived there for the next twelve years.

They brought to their new home a profound dedication to "Peace on Earth", human dignity, justice, and diversity. International activists, with their three children grown and on their own, the big house soon filled with visitors and students from around the world. The hillside house became a hostel, haven and think-tank for people coming to the Philadelphia area through its Center for International Visitors. Once isolated and parochial, the farm now found the world coming to its door.

Their benevolent hospitality was most noticeable at Christmastime. The children, and soon grandchildren, returned to spend time in the embracing warmth of fireplace blazes stoked by wood Ben cut in the neighboring farmer's woodlot.

Regional Director of the National Labor Relations Board, woodcutting was Ben's release from the demands of negotiating, a spiritual exercise that everyone recognized and respected. There were times when he, like Thoreau, had to "go to the woods". Christmas Day was no exception.

Like shepherds gathering sheep far from their own flock into a safe enclosure, the Schaufflers and the old house, hosted foreign guests at their holiday table. They shared their family's Yuletide traditions and probably learned many from other lands.

The tree was trimmed, but never with electric lights. Sometimes real candles were risked reminding me how remarkable it is that the house has survived so many tapers, oil lamps, and fireplace cinders. Stockings were hung, a family activity of exceptional importance according to Jing, and favorite games played.

During quieter moments, there was talk of the Korean War, nuclear proliferation, and McCarthy's anti-Communist crusade in the Senate. The house's walls have absorbed accounts of so many milestones in the country's history and heard so many differing views over the years. How I long to unlock their impenetrable, stony silence. I wish I could hear it all.

In the early 1960's Marnie and Ben found it was time to "downsize." Wanting smaller, less demanding quarters, they returned to the tenant house. They subdivided the building and two acres from the main parcel selling the "Big House" and eight acres to my husband, Howard, and me. They were our neighbors for a number of years and we admired their continuing vitality and interest in world affairs. The echo of Ben's axe being laid to wood all around our small valley was as beloved a sound as lowing cows, purring tractors and the hum of Howard's beehives.

At Christmas I am thankful for the tendrils of good will that reached out to the world from this house during the Schauffler's time here.

Christmas in the 1960's

It was music that brought Howard and me to this beautiful hillside home, and specifically, to Dallas and John's unfinished museum. For the next 26 years both would be at the heart of all the Christmases celebrated here.

We named the farmhouse Burnswark after an ancestral family home in Ecclefechan, Scotland.

A church organist and pipe organ architect, Howard sought a house with a room large enough to build the sizeable pipe organ he had always wanted. Being, as well, an architectural designer specializing in colonial revivalism, he preferred an early house that would satisfy our mutual love of Pennsylvania vernacular architecture. Like Dallas and John, when the realtor brought us to the property, we knew instantly that it fulfilled all our requirements. The Cottage was perfect for the music room, the house and its bucolic surroundings for rearing children and living a simple, rural life.

We moved in the spring of 1962, bringing our Black Labrador, Queenie, Golden Retriever, Clem, and several cats. We looked forward to having many domestic and semi-domestic animals, and immediately enlarged our menagerie with four noisy, opinionated Emden geese, the kind that often highlight holiday meals, (but would never grace *our* table).

Our initial Christmas was spent in a sparsely furnished house, and with the outdoors pervaded by continual commotion caused

"I'm dreaming of a white Christmas,
Just like the ones I used to know,
Where the treetops glisten and children listen
To hear sleigh bells in the snow..."

–IRVING BERLIN

by dogs, cats and geese trying to figure out who was in charge; an activity complicated by a substantial snowfall requiring all to maneuver with more than the usual agility. It was chaotically comical causing consternation in Burnswark's visitors as well as its occupants.

That our first Christmas was white made it particularly memorable. We loved everything about winter; the way wood smoke rises straight as an arrow from the chimney when the air is cold and still, the strange silence of a snowstorm, the black silhouette of trees against a blazing winter sunset.

Living at Burnswark heightened these sentiments. The old house seemed to enfold and protect us like a mother's arms or a father's lap.

It's stone walls did not shake when the wind blew and low ceilings preserved warmth.

Little windows shut out the elements, but framed winter's vistas like pictures hanging on the walls.

The large walk-in fireplaces invited us to sit beside them, and we knew they could warm and feed us should modern conveniences fail in a storm.

O little town of Bethlehem
How still we see thee lie.
Above thy deep and dreamless sleep,
The silent stars go by;
Yet in thy dark streets shineth
The everlasting light.
The hopes and fears of all the years
Are met in thee tonight.

-Phillips Brooks

We noticed the unique way candle and Christmas light reflected off the uneven white-washed walls. They glowed with muted yellows, oranges and reds. Even dark corners radiated warmth with soft brown rather than cold, black hues.

We came to treasure this subdued yet shimmering luminosity, especially at Christmastime.

Five years passed before the Cottage was converted into our longed-for music room. Meanwhile, Howard's Steinway Concert Grand piano was placed in the living room, where, with the fireplace, it "held court" leaving little room for furniture.

Here, we planned and rehearsed music for Christmas services at church, and, as the holidays drew near, invited friends for caroling around the piano. At the fireplace, Howard served spiced wine and rum heated in a copper kettle hanging from the trammel bar, a tradition that continued throughout our years together.

On Christmas Eve we trimmed the tree and set up the family crèche while eating by the fire, often in great haste. Leaving promptly for the 11 o'clock service always took precedence over other activities. But the service and its music were the center of our Christmas celebration, and we looked forward to our departure with genuine excitement.

The drive home after church, in the first dark hour of Christmas Day, included some of our most cherished Yuletide moments, a quiet interlude bracketed by holiday activities completed, and those that would resume in the morning. Leaving the suburbs behind, we headed west toward the countryside of the Chester Valley. Topping the ridge, we could see, even in dead of night, its hills and meadows spreading before us, lying in "deep and dreamless sleep" under starry skies. The blackness was speckled with lights of outdoor Christmas trees and the windows of a few widely scattered homes. It was a diorama of exquisite, peaceful beauty. Somehow feeling that we were driving through a holy space, we would alternate between respectful silence and quiet song:

"From heaven on high to earth I come,
To bring good news to every home.
Glad tidings of great joy I bring,
Whereof I now shall say and sing..."

-MARTIN LUTHER

71

"Silent night, Holy night, all is calm, all is bright....."

-HANS GRUEBER

Light from the house greeted us as we drove up the snowy lane. We navigated our way to the door rather circuitously, trying to avoid the nips of the geese that, made irritable by the cold, were having more than the usual trouble remembering that we were the people they were supposed to be protecting.

Reaching the safety of the porch, we paused to glance skyward remembering Christmas Eves when we were young and longed to catch a glimpse of Santa's sleigh. But recent events required that we look at the heavens with more than the usual awe, for it was in the sky that year history had been made and then almost ended.

1962 marked the beginning of the Space Age. America had launched three astronauts into outer space and sent probes to Venus and Mercury. It seemed incredible that just 75 years earlier, the Lewises, and most of mankind, had relied only on horses and a few steam engines to get about. As we gazed at those Christmas morning stars we never imagined that, in seven years, Americans would walk on the moon.

Two months earlier, had things not turned out as they did, the same beautiful sky might have rained nuclear devastation down upon us and, through retaliation, the rest of the world; effectively ending history. For many days that October, the Cuban Missile Crisis held us on the brink of disaster.

So we stood there in the dark, on our farmhouse porch, sensing the solid, comforting protection of the old building we were about to enter, and gratefully looking forward to the sun rising on another Christmas Day.

The remaining years of the decade were happy ones. We gave Burnswark a fresh coat of paint, made improvements to some of her architectural elements, bought antiques, laid out flowerbeds and a vegetable garden, added a basset hound to our complement of dogs, and acquired a crate full of bantam chickens from auction. The crate turned out to contain significantly more roosters than hens giving new meaning to the phrase "the cock crew".

Christmas 1967 was joyfully unforgettable due to the birth of our first son, Spencer, and the completion of the music room and pipe organ. Throughout the season, Howard

73

"Break forth O beauteous heavenly light, And usher in the morning..."

FROM THE
CHRISTMAS ORATORIO
— J.S. BACH

often took his new son to the organ, where he played the great Christmas chorus from Handel's <u>Messiah</u> for him.

"For unto us a child is born,
unto us a son is given,
And the government shall be upon
his shoulders,
And his name shall be called,
Wonderful, Councilor,
The mighty God, the everlasting
Father, the Prince of Peace..."

The baby added another dimension to our holidays as childhood re-entered our lives. We had nearly forgotten how much we missed it, how exciting it is to view Christmas through youthful eyes. Santa Claus would be back with stockings and toy trains, trucks, puzzles and games. We hadn't really outgrown them. They had merely been put away in a corner of our lives, along with other childlike pleasures marked "inactive". Now they were out again for the three of us to share through all the Christmases that lay ahead.

Between Christmases, our attention focused on the enormous social and political tidal waves that were rocking the Ship of State: collapsing family traditions, assassination, Vietnam, the struggle for Civil Rights. Through church and political involvement we became increasingly active, striving to do our share as members of the crew.

By the decade's final Christmas, we allowed ourselves to believe that, somehow, unconsciously, the truths spoken by the angels were being drawn upon to fashion the changes underway. Good will among men could start with justice; Peace on Earth by avoiding wars.

"He spake, and straightway the celestial choir
In hymns of joy unknown before, conspire;
....God's highest glory was their anthem still,
Peace on the earth, and unto men good will."

-JOHN BYROM, 1749

Christmas in the 1970's

Throughout the first Christmas season of the 1970's we celebrated the addition of our second son, Edward, to our family circle. Now two stockings hung above Jacob Baum's great fireplace, and another "engineer" was available to help plan the little village and miniature trains under the tree. And yes, Howard took him to the organ and played "For unto us a child is born, unto us a son is given!".

Caroling had become an annual event, and the numbers of participants increased, filling the house to capacity. First, a brief rehearsal was held at the organ followed by a visit to the hearth for a cup of mulled wine or eggnog and a sampling of cheese fondue and fruit. Then all bundled warmly, we took candles from a box by the door, and headed into the night on our Yuletide trek through the countryside.

In those days, we had few neighbors, but the long walk between houses was as enjoyable as the doorway caroling itself. As eyes adjusted to the darkness we could see valleys, hills, and horizons in all directions, and lights from homes dotting the vistas. Warmly sequestered in their barns, cows intermittently called to us; the sound quietly ricocheting from ridge to hollow.

When there was no wind candles were lit, and we walked in twos and threes, strung out along the road like a garland. Occasionally singing as we went, the front of the line was always a beat or two ahead of the rear, giving the music an echoing quality.

"Calm on the listening ear of night,
Comes heaven's melodious strains,
Where wild Judea stretches far
Her silver mantled plains..."

-Edward Hamilton Sears (Hymn 24)

Our destination was the tiny village of Lyndell, where a group of houses clustered around the country store near the covered bridge that spanned the Brandywine Creek. It was to the small railroad depot there, that Henry Lewis and Isaac Hall had delivered their milk for shipment to market in years past.

Several older couples lived in the little community. A note we received touchingly illustrates their appreciation of our efforts.

"...It was such a surprise when I opened the door, seeing the moving figures with candles coming into the light of the porch from the dark road. We had never witnessed anything similar in our lives. To listen to the unusually beautiful singing by a large group under expert direction was an experience long to remember.

To be able to gather so many volunteers to travel a distance to sing or us in the village was inspiring. Then we saw something-also inspiring- you yourselves could not see. From our window we saw the tiny lights of the candles in a line as you were passing up the Creek Road, and later, returning. That was a sight never seen before in these parts.

....We wish to apologize for not outwardly saying more in appreciation. I never had such a feeling of the meaning of Christmas, especially since it had come at the close of a hectic day of frustration with problems that seemed to mar the Christmas spirit.

You folks changed that attitude to meaningful thoughts to begin the Holiday season in a way never to be forgotten by us. Happy New Year..."

Returning home, Burnswark's lighted windows beckoned. Cold but happy, we looked forward to hot soup, warm wine and more music within.

There, around the organ, those with special talents performed on their instruments, and individuals, or the group, sang favorite anthems and carols.

A friend's aging mother visiting from Munich sang, in a yet pure voice, "Silent Night" in German. Our cousin, a tenor, led us in the canon "Non Nobis Dominum". The choir's first soprano, joined by her husband, a flutist, performed "He shall Feed His Flock" from Messiah.

The evening usually ended with Howard reading the Christmas Lesson from St. John:

"In the beginning was the word,
And the word was with God, and the
Word was God.....",

followed by all singing Handel's Hallelujah Chorus.

Often during those gatherings, I would think of the McCrosky sisters, and wonder if they could hear the music filling their little wilderness home.

Christmas Eve day and evening were the most exciting of the holidays, particularly for the children. The pleasure of anticipation is never more palpable than it is during those twenty-four hours.

Two Past Twelve

Standing like a totem in the hall,
Does it know
What day it just announced?
As the hands pass twelve,
Does it perceive
That there is something
Different
In the hours,
Minutes, seconds,
It will count off
Until it next strikes midnight?

Being old, its hands have marked
The entrance of two hundred
Christmas morns.
And yet its countenance,
Seemingly as immune to partiality

As Lady Justice, (though not as blind),
Reveals no special mood
Or recognition.
Its painted face stares out above our eyes,
Not looking at the darkened room or us,
But to the future.

No festive crescendo embellishes
Its Yuletide chime.
The heartbeat of its pendulum
Does not quicken.
Tick.....Tick.....Tick. . . . .

Yet we, whose hours
It stoically records,
Hear, this night, its midnight striking
With delight.

The bell, whose timbre
Other days is simple declaration,
To ears that listen now
Is proclamation and
A heralding!

"Welcome Christmas!"
Once again, in dead of night,
You slip into our lives.
Advancing through the hall,
Passing the clock,
It overlooks you
As you proceed to other rooms.

When hands reach six
And morning barely gilds the sky,

Amidst the tick and tock
Come little footsteps over
creaking boards;
Whispers, laughter, and sleepy
"Merry Christmases",
Punctured by a yawn or two.

Then down the stairs come one
And all,
Passing their hallway sentinel,
Which is at work
Counting the minutes to
The next Yuletide's midnight song.
Tick.....Tick.....Tick.

-KATHARINE OKIE

82

Like every other day, Christmas morning was heralded by the chaotic cacophony of our rooster choir, each trying to outdo the other with cracking, hoarse voices caused by cold air. The chicken coop's inability to adequately house our out-of-control bantam population resulted in many of them roosting in the apple tree outside our bedroom window. Like Isaac Hall, we found the slaughtering solution repugnant since we knew each of them, and rather enjoyed their display of irrational impudence. Along with the geese and our Bassett Hound, they also made us laugh. Anyhow, we could never catch them.

The next sounds we heard were the children's footsteps running toward our door, followed by two little knocks. In winter the old floorboards creaked more than usual and each had its own pitch and timbre. After a while we came to know which sound went with which board in which room. It was really quite companionable; as though the house were talking to us. There were several very loud boards in the hall between the children's rooms and ours, so we could always hear them coming. But the noise they made on Christmas morning was different from all the rest because the children *jumped* off the two little steps leading to the hall, and then *ran* across the floor to our room. I will never forget the sound of that joyful Christmas morning dash, in a house that couldn't keep it a secret.

Downstairs, we opened stockings by the hearth, and the boys always marveled at the wood-ash footprints leading from the fireplace to the table where they had left milk and cookies. When they were young, the walk-in fire-place that received the jolly old elf intrigued the children. It must have seemed like a big, dark cave and I often found one or the other inside, playing with a little car or truck. As they walked out they left a wood-ash trail like Santa did on Christmas Eve.

Certain packages under the tree always stood out from the rest. These were the ones Howard wrapped in the color comic section of the newspaper. It seemed odd to me until I learned its origins. His father was a "country" lawyer, sometimes serving his poorer clients pro bono. The Depression had been particularly hard on him, and when Christmas came, there sometimes was little under the tree. What was there was wrapped in the comics, an exercise in thrift that was a family hallmark. Howard

never forgot those few, modestly concealed gifts. Like other Depression-era children, he had learned the number of presents one received had little to do with a meaningful Christmas. Living as we were in a time of increasing holiday commercialism, it was his way of keeping things in perspective.

Late in the afternoon, on our return from church and Christmas dinner with family, we completed the enjoyable task of opening packages, which was always cut short in the morning by our dash to Christmas Day services. Our dogs and cats joined us, and we wondered if the ghosts of other pets, long gone, were also in the room. There must have been many over the years. If they were as much a part of their households as our animals are, they were hovering nearby in some favorite spot that had been especially theirs.

While the children played with new toys, we continued conversations that had been started at Christmas dinner, from moonwalks to Watergate. Sometimes there were things to celebrate, sometimes not. Burnswark's old walls just listened.

During Christmas of 1974 our fireplaces and woodstoves kept us warm when the country was gripped by oil shortages caused by an Arab embargo. Sitting around the hearth that Christmas was more a necessity than a nostalgic pastime.

We celebrated the Bicentennial in 1976 as the Lewises had observed the Centennial one hundred years earlier. Burnswark had shepherded its families through another century of holidays with quiet, unobtrusive care.

Christmas at the end of the Second Millenium

$\mathcal{A}$S WE ENTERED THE 1980's, the decade made famous by George Orwell novels, our lives were singularly un-futuristic. We were enriched by the quiet, rural life Burnswark offered us, and literally surrounded by the farming activities of our neighbor's dairy enterprise, allowing us to vicariously enjoy the business of agriculture.

Their large Holstein herd visited us each day in the meadow in front of the house, and we watched as they were called to the upper farm for milking in the evening. We saw crops being planted, harvested and stored; and calves being born.

The sounds of farming heralded changing seasons as much as the song of Red-winged blackbirds in spring, or the call of the Blue

Jays in the fall. After a long winter, waking to hear the drone of the tractor plowing early in the morning literally made our hearts leap, and simultaneously say to each other, "Spring is here!" We would promptly go outside to rake, plant and tend our own gardens.

After a seemingly endless, hot summer, the first muffled roar of the combine, and the rattle of the grain elevator let us know fall was coming after all, setting us to cutting wood and mulching flower beds.

When headlights from a tractor far out in the field until well past nine o'clock, supplemented light from October's huge harvest moon, we knew planting winter wheat signaled colder days, and the approach of the holidays.

Farming necessities sometimes affected Christmas Day itself. In warm, rainy years,

The tree of life my soul hath seen,
Laden with fruit and always green...
...This fruit doth make
my soul to thrive....
..It keeps my dying faith alive,
Which makes my soul in haste to be
With Jesus Christ,
the Apple Tree....

-1784 NEW ENGLAND CAROL

the farmer spreading accumulated droppings from the barn to advantage resulted in the jarringly unique combination of manure 's odor mingling with the scents of balsam fir and candy canes.

During the rest of the year the same pastoral surroundings provided a peaceful buffer from the concerns of a challenging, confusing time. The American culture continued to reinvent itself and, like progress in any era, each revision had positive and negative elements. Thinking them through could be stressful. The disparity between the values of the popular culture and those of the family became more pronounced, and concern about the health of the environment was heightening.

But Christmas gave the nation, and us, a time to regroup, returning to traditions most people still cherished. The music, the tree, the family gatherings and the message remained relevant and uplifting; themes of love and tolerance holding family members and friends of differing views together. Burnswark itself provided a sense of continuity. Sitting restfully on its hillside, her old windows seemed to gaze at us reassuringly.

Two important milestones marked the final Christmases of the '80's, one sorrowful for our family, one joyful for the world.

In July of 1988 Howard died after a year-long illness. Our sons, now teenagers, and I struggled with the reality of our loss, particularly at Christmas. The vacuum of silence in the music room and our lives that December was heart wrenching. But as with the Baum's after Jacob's death, and the Lewises after

Heap on more wood! —the wind is chill;
But let it whistle as it will,
We'll keep our Christmas merry still.
Each age has deem'd the newborn year
The fittest time for festal cheer.

-SIR WALTER SCOTT

Henry's, Christmas itself helped us adjust to life without him. The tree, the decorating, the music (via our stereo), continued. The gift of life kept on giving, and over time, the happiness of the season returned to Burnswark's hearths.

Internationally, Peace on Earth was given another chance when the fifty year Cold War ended, a gift to mankind of enormous magnitude.

As Ann Lewis had 89 years earlier, I turned my attention to making plans enabling me to stay at Burnswark as a widow. Remembering the Hall's leased rooms to help them through the Depression, and feeling Burnswark's 19th century ambiance made it suitable for a Bed and Breakfast, I undertook some renovations, and opened the Lewis wing to guests.

The music room was another source of rental space. Sorrowfully, I sold the organ to make room for a kitchen, bath and closets. After 177 years the McCrosky sisters' little cottage was to become a home again. To my delight, the new tenants were my son Edward, his wife Jennifer, and, after several years, their baby son, Callum. Seeing his crib in the place the organ's huge pipes had stood turned the pain of change and loss into the joy of change and gain.

Shortly after opening the B & B, I rented one of the rooms to my nephew William who, with Edward, had done the renovations. He brought his dog, Trail Mix, and they stayed for the next 10 years, becoming an integral part of life at Burnswark.

Christmas filled the house with family throughout the 1990's. Son Spencer, his wife Renee, their daughter's Angelica and Desiree, nephews and nieces, sister, in- laws, Mother, Father and friends put the B & B guestrooms to good use. The door connecting the Cottage Apartment was opened allowing people to flow from one end of the long house to the other as they had during caroling party days. The ability of the old house to adapt to the needs of the moment always amazed me. It seemed to be breathing, exhaling and inhaling, expanding and contracting, always keeping things close, cozy, and convenient with its unpretentious holiday hospitality.

As December 31, 1999 approached, there was widespread concern that a programming error in computers might interpret the year '00 as 1900 rather than 2000, causing a worldwide shut down, bringing everything to a standstill. Many, including me, chose to stay home that New Year's Eve in case the prediction proved accurate. But should the worst occur, I knew the hallway grandfather clock would keep on ticking, water could be gotten from the springhouse, food cooked and the house heated by the fireplaces. Thankfully, midnight came and went without so much as a flicker of the lights.

God bless the master of this house,
Likewise the mistress too,
And all the little children
that round the table go!
Love and joy come to you,
And to you, your wassail too,
And God bless you, and send you
A happy New Year!
And God send you
A happy New Year!

THE WASSAIL SONG

I walked out onto the porch and welcomed the new millennium by ringing the farm bell. There were many more lights surrounding the hill now, for the affluence of the last decade had drawn suburbia to the area, and most of the farms were gone. For a few moments I felt a vivid bond with Burnswark's families. They, and Howard, seemed to be with me, watching the same stars we had all viewed at different times over the past two, remarkable centuries. Before going inside, I sent silent good wishes to them, to those whose home it would be in the future.

"For lo! The days are hastening on,
By prophets seen of old,
When with the ever-circling years
Shall come the time foretold,
When peace shall over all the earth

Its ancient splendors fling,
And the whole world give back the song
Which now the angels sing."

-E<small>DMUND</small> H. S<small>EARS</small>

When I return home after being out for the day, I am always happy to see Burnswark nestled on the side of the hill, waiting for me. It isn't modern or filled with gadgets and conveniences, particularly closets. It wasn't designed to impress, promote, or make a spectacle of itself. It was built for solid, reliable, shelter; to give its occupants a sense of tranquility and protection, and after two hundred years, it is continues to be an ideal place in which to live, think, and grow.

When Christmas comes, I am equally glad to experience its familiar, inspiring tradi-

tions in an age of new customs and startling events. It is not a festival that celebrates power, wealth, or self-absorption. It honors humility, generosity, selflessness; after two thousand years, it continues to be an ideal season for living, thinking, and growing.

The house and the holiday are well matched.

Twelfth Night

Where did it go-
That long awaited season
We invest with such
Anticipation?
It brought us sparkling moments:
Prisms of beauty that appeared
Unexpectedly,
And flashed by,
Sprinkling us with Christmas dust.

It was the time to be
A child again;
Filled with childlike hopes and trust,
And faith untarnished by
The questions cynics ask.
I felt again the truth of every promise
I had dreamed when I was young;
And glad because those dreams were good,

And some were done.
The two-edged gifts of choice,
The need to scrutinize,
Were laid aside.
We reveled in an ancient tale;
That is, quite simply,
All we need to know.
(Not an equation, or a binary code,)
Just a phrase some angels sang
Long, long ago:
"Good will, Good will,
Good will toward men!".

So I linger by this Yuletide hearth,
Bedecked with greens and candlelight.
While brass and copper shining bright
Reflect a hundred Christmas nights
Of years gone by.

Balsam's fragrance roams the room,
A welcome friend,
Blending with apple, cinnamon, and mint,
Pausing at each corner
And beside my chair.

Sweet, well-loved music
Plies my heart
With halo-ed memories
Not letting me forget the gift of
Its familiarity.
Relinquishing such peace
Is hard to do.
I hold on, resisting its departure
As I would a child's
Who I know is old enough to go on
Without me.

But go it must.
From the child's hand

I take an added measure of
Good will
And place it in my pocket.

Now the infant New Year cries
For my attention.
It and I will wake, blossom,
Flower, age together.
And, side by side, withering,
Some twelve months hence,
Raise our graying heads again
To hear the angels sing.

-KATHARINE OKIE

NOW..."May your days be merry
and bright. And may all your
Christmases be white."

-IRVING BERLIN

96